Unstoppable Entrepreneur: Strategies for Overcoming Adversity and Achieving Success

Rashed Saqer Obaid Al Dhaheri

Table of Contents

List of Figures

Foreword

Entrepreneurship is a challenging and rewarding journey, but it can also be a difficult one. The road to success is littered with obstacles and setbacks, and it takes a special kind of person to overcome them and achieve success. That special kind of person is an unstoppable entrepreneur.

An unstoppable entrepreneur is someone who possesses the mindset, attitude, and skills necessary to overcome adversity and achieve success. They are resilient, adaptable, and innovative, and they possess the leadership and team-building skills necessary to build and manage high-performing teams.

This book is a guide for entrepreneurs who are looking to develop the mindset, attitude, and skills necessary to become unstoppable. It provides practical strategies and techniques for developing a growth mindset, cultivating a positive attitude, setting and achieving goals, managing risks, building a strong support system, developing resilience and adaptability, fostering innovation and creativity, building and managing high-performing teams, and developing effective marketing and sales strategies.

The book is divided into eight sections, each of which focuses on a different aspect of the unstoppable entrepreneur mindset. The first section provides an introduction to the concept of the unstoppable entrepreneur and the importance of overcoming adversity in entrepreneurship.

The second section focuses on mindset and attitude, and provides strategies for developing a growth mindset, cultivating a positive attitude, and overcoming limiting beliefs.

The third section focuses on planning and preparation, and provides strategies for setting and achieving goals, identifying and managing risks, and building a strong support system.

The fourth section focuses on resilience and adaptability, and provides strategies for developing resilience in the face of failure, learning from mistakes and setbacks, and adapting to change and uncertainty.

The fifth section focuses on innovation and creativity, and provides strategies for encouraging innovation and out-of-the-box thinking, leveraging technology and digital tools, and cultivating a culture of creativity.

The sixth section focuses on leadership and team building, and provides strategies for developing leadership skills, building and managing high-performing teams, and fostering effective communication and collaboration.

The seventh section focuses on sales and marketing, and provides strategies for understanding and reaching your target market, building and maintaining a strong brand, and developing effective marketing strategies.

The eighth section provides a conclusion, summarizing key takeaways from the book and providing a final call to action for readers.

This book is a must-read for any entrepreneur who wants to develop the mindset, attitude, and skills necessary to become unstoppable. It provides practical strategies and techniques that can be applied immediately, and it is a valuable resource for entrepreneurs at any stage of their journey. Whether you are just starting out or are a seasoned entrepreneur, this book will provide you with the tools and strategies you need to overcome adversity and achieve success.

This book provides the guidance and support you need to develop the mindset, attitude, and skills necessary to overcome adversity and achieve success in the face of uncertainty and change. I highly recommend it to any entrepreneur who is looking to take business to the next level.

Dedication

With humble gratitude, I dedicate this book to His Highness Sheikh Mohammed Bin Zayed Al Nahyan, the President of the United Arab Emirates. His unwavering commitment to making the UAE a hub for innovation and a model for the world has been the source of my inspiration in writing this book.

As a leader, HH Sheikh Mohammed Bin Zayed has shown a deep understanding of the changing global landscape and the importance of knowledge-based economies in the 21st century. His vision to move the UAE away from an oil-based economy and towards a future that is driven by ideas, creativity, and technology has been nothing short of remarkable.

I am thankful to the leadership of the UAE for creating an environment that supports entrepreneurship, creativity and personal growth. The country's investments in education, technology, and infrastructure have made it a top destination for the brightest minds from around the world.

This book is a tribute to the visionary leadership of HH Sheikh Mohammed Bin Zayed and a celebration of the limitless potential of the UAE. May this nation continue to shine as a beacon of hope and progress for generations to come!

Who Should Read This Book?

This book is ideal for anyone who is interested in entrepreneurship, from aspiring entrepreneurs who are just starting out to experienced business owners who are looking to take their ventures to the next level.

The book is also relevant for individuals who are considering starting a business but are unsure of how to navigate the challenges and opportunities of entrepreneurship. The expected benefits of reading this book include:

1) A better understanding of what it takes to become an unstoppable entrepreneur, including strategies for overcoming adversity and achieving success.

2) An increased awareness of the importance of developing a growth mindset, cultivating a positive attitude, and overcoming limiting beliefs.

3) A deeper understanding of the importance of planning and preparation, including setting and achieving goals, identifying and managing risks, and building a strong support system.

4) A clearer understanding of the importance of resilience and adaptability in entrepreneurship, including developing resilience in the face of failure, learning from mistakes and setbacks, and adapting to change and uncertainty.

5) An improved ability to encourage innovation and out-of-the-box thinking, leverage technology and digital tools, and cultivate a culture of creativity.

6) An enhanced understanding of the importance of leadership and team building, including developing leadership skills and building and managing high-performing teams.

7) A deeper understanding of the importance of sales and marketing for entrepreneurs, including understanding and reaching your target market,

building and maintaining a strong brand, and developing effective marketing strategies.

8) An improved ability to navigate complex regulations and political systems and leverage technology and data to make informed decisions.

Overall, this book is a valuable resource for anyone who wants to start a business or improve their current entrepreneurial ventures. By reading this book, individuals can gain a deeper understanding of the strategies and concepts that are crucial for success in entrepreneurship and be well-equipped to navigate the challenges and opportunities of the future.

Chapter I

Introduction

Entrepreneurship is a challenging and rewarding journey, but it can also be a difficult one. The road to success is littered with obstacles and setbacks, and it takes a special kind of person to overcome them and achieve success. That special kind of person is an unstoppable entrepreneur. Before that I would like to define an entrepreneur.

An entrepreneur is an individual who starts, organizes, and manages a new business venture. They take on financial risks in order to start and grow a business. They are responsible for the overall direction and success of the business. Entrepreneurs are often characterized by their ability to identify opportunities, create and innovate new products or services, and manage resources effectively. They also possess leadership, strategic thinking and problem solving skills, and are able to navigate uncertainty and change. They are often driven by a passion to create something new and the desire to be their own boss.

But what exactly is an unstoppable entrepreneur? An unstoppable entrepreneur is someone who possesses the mindset, attitude, and skills necessary to overcome adversity and achieve success. They are resilient, adaptable, and innovative, and they possess the leadership and team-building skills necessary to build and manage high-performing teams.

An unstoppable entrepreneur is someone who is not deterred by failure, but rather uses it as an opportunity to learn and grow. They are able to see challenges as opportunities for improvement and growth, rather than obstacles to be avoided. They possess a positive attitude, an ability to think strategically, and the ability to inspire others to join them on their journey.

The importance of overcoming adversity in entrepreneurship cannot be overstated. Entrepreneurship is a risky and uncertain endeavour, and it is impossible to avoid all obstacles and setbacks. However, an unstoppable entrepreneur is able to face these challenges head-on and overcome them. They are able to adapt to changing circumstances and find new opportunities in the face of adversity.

Overcoming adversity requires a growth mindset, which is the belief that one's abilities and intelligence can be developed through effort and learning. An entrepreneur with a growth mindset is able to see failure as an opportunity to learn and grow, rather than as a setback. They are also able to view challenges as opportunities for improvement and growth.

In addition to a growth mindset, an unstoppable entrepreneur also possesses a positive attitude and the ability to think strategically. They are able to maintain a positive outlook, even in the face of adversity.

This positive attitude allows them to see opportunities and possibilities, even when others see only challenges and obstacles. They can think strategically and make informed decisions that help them achieve success.

An unstoppable entrepreneur also possesses the leadership and team-building skills necessary to build and manage high-performing teams. They are able to inspire and motivate others to join them on their journey. They are able to communicate effectively and foster collaboration and teamwork. They are able to build a strong support system that helps them overcome adversity and achieve success.

Whether you are just starting out or are a seasoned entrepreneur, this book will provide you with the tools and strategies you need to overcome adversity and achieve success. It is a valuable resource for entrepreneurs at any stage of their journey, and it will help you develop the mindset, attitude, and skills necessary to become an unstoppable entrepreneur.

Who is an unstoppable entrepreneur

An unstoppable entrepreneur is someone who possesses the mindset, attitude, and skills necessary to overcome adversity and achieve success. They are resilient, adaptable, and innovative, and they possess the leadership and team-building skills necessary to build and manage high-performing teams.

An unstoppable entrepreneur is someone who is not deterred by failure, but rather uses it as an opportunity to learn and grow. They are able to see challenges as opportunities for improvement and growth, rather than obstacles to be avoided. They possess a positive attitude, an ability to think strategically, and the ability to inspire others to join them on their journey.

One of the key characteristics of an unstoppable entrepreneur is their growth mindset. A growth mindset is the belief that one's abilities and intelligence can be developed through effort and learning. An entrepreneur with a growth mindset is able to see failure as an opportunity to learn and grow, rather than as a setback.

They are also able to view challenges as opportunities for improvement and growth. This mindset enables them to approach problems and setbacks with a positive and proactive attitude.

An unstoppable entrepreneur also possesses a positive attitude and the ability to think strategically. They are able to maintain a positive outlook, even in the face of adversity.

This positive attitude allows them to see opportunities and possibilities, even when others see only challenges and obstacles. They can think strategically and make informed decisions that help them achieve success.

An unstoppable entrepreneur is also someone who is adaptable and able to navigate uncertainty and change. They are able to pivot and adjust their strategies as needed in response to changing market conditions or unforeseen obstacles.

They are able to think outside the box and come up with innovative solutions to problems. They are able to take calculated risks and make bold moves when necessary.

Another important characteristic of an unstoppable entrepreneur is their ability to build and maintain a strong personal brand. They understand the importance of creating a strong and consistent brand message that resonates with their target market. They are able to leverage social media and other digital tools to promote their brand and connect with potential customers.

In addition to these characteristics, an unstoppable entrepreneur is also someone who is constantly learning and seeking out new knowledge and skills. They understand that in order to stay ahead in the ever-changing business landscape, they must constantly be learning and adapting.

They seek out mentorship and guidance from more experienced entrepreneurs, attend industry conferences and events, and read industry-related books and publications. They also make it a priority to keep up with new technologies, trends and best practices in their field.

An unstoppable entrepreneur is characterized by their unyielding mindset, optimistic outlook, strategic thinking abilities, and leadership skills needed to lead and manage successful teams. These attributes equip them to tackle challenges and attain success.

They are adaptable and able to navigate uncertainty and change, and they are able to build and maintain a strong personal brand. An unstoppable entrepreneur is always learning, seeking out new knowledge and skills and staying ahead in the ever-changing business landscape.

It is important to note that being an unstoppable entrepreneur is not something that one is born with, it is something that can be developed. With the right mindset, attitude and skills, anyone can become an unstoppable entrepreneur. Here is a summary of key characteristics of an unstoppable entrepreneur:

1) An unstoppable entrepreneur is someone who possesses the mindset, attitude, and skills necessary to overcome adversity and achieve success. They possess a growth mindset, a positive attitude, and the ability to think strategically. They are resilient, adaptable, and innovative, and possess the leadership and team-building skills necessary to build and manage high-performing teams.

2) An unstoppable entrepreneur is one who embraces failure and uses it as a learning opportunity to grow and improve. They have a positive attitude, strong leadership skills, and the ability to adapt and pivot

when necessary. They have a clear vision, and the drive and determination to make it a reality.

3) An unstoppable entrepreneur is an individual who is not deterred by obstacles, but rather embraces them as opportunities for growth. They possess a growth mindset, a positive attitude, and the ability to think strategically. They have strong leadership and team-building skills, and they are able to navigate uncertainty and change with ease.

4) An unstoppable entrepreneur is a person who possesses the resilience, adaptability and determination to overcome adversity and achieve success. They have a growth mindset, a positive attitude and the ability to think strategically. They have strong leadership, team building skills and the ability to inspire others to join them on their journey.

5) An unstoppable entrepreneur is an individual who has the ability to think strategically, the leadership skills to build and manage high-performing teams, and the resilience and adaptability to overcome adversity and achieve success. They have a growth mindset, a positive attitude, and the ability to

navigate uncertainty and change with ease. They are innovative, and possess the drive and determination to make their vision a reality.

Here are a few examples of real-life entrepreneurs who can be considered "unstoppable":

Elon Musk - The CEO of Tesla and SpaceX, Elon Musk is a prime example of an unstoppable entrepreneur. He has faced numerous setbacks and obstacles throughout his career, but he has always found a way to overcome them and achieve success. He has a growth mindset, always learning from his failures and using them to improve. Musk is known for his ability to think strategically, and his ability to inspire and motivate others to join him on his journey.

Oprah Winfrey - Oprah Winfrey is a media mogul and entrepreneur who has faced numerous challenges throughout her career. She faced poverty, abuse, and discrimination early in her life, but she used these experiences to become a stronger and more resilient person. Winfrey has a positive attitude and the ability to think strategically, which has helped her overcome adversity and achieve success. She is a great example of an unstoppable entrepreneur who has built a strong support system and has the ability to inspire others.

Mark Zuckerberg - The founder and CEO of Facebook, Mark Zuckerberg is another example of an unstoppable entrepreneur. He started Facebook while still a student at Harvard, and has faced numerous challenges and obstacles throughout his career. He has a growth mindset and a positive attitude, which has helped him overcome adversity and achieve success. He is a great example of an entrepreneur who has the ability to think strategically, and has the leadership skills necessary to build and manage high-performing teams.

Sara Blakely - The founder of Spanx, Sara Blakely is a great example of an unstoppable entrepreneur. She started her company with just $5,000, and has faced numerous challenges and setbacks throughout her journey. She has a growth mindset, and she always saw opportunities in the face of adversity. Blakely is known for her positive attitude and her ability to think strategically, which has helped her overcome adversity and achieve success.

These are just a few examples of real-life entrepreneurs who can be considered "unstoppable". These entrepreneurs have faced many challenges and obstacles throughout their journey, but they have been able to overcome them and achieve success.

They have a growth mindset, a positive attitude, the ability to think strategically, and the leadership skills necessary to build and manage high-performing teams. They are great examples of how an unstoppable entrepreneur mindset works.

The importance of overcoming adversity

Adversity can be defined as a difficult or unpleasant situation or circumstance, such as a setback, obstacle, or challenge. It can refer to a wide range of situations, from financial difficulties and market fluctuations, to personal and professional setbacks, to natural disasters and other unexpected events.

Adversity can be short term or long term and can have a significant impact on an individual or a business. It is an inevitable part of life and in the case of entrepreneurship it can be especially challenging as it can threaten the viability of the business and the livelihood of the entrepreneur.

The importance of overcoming adversity in entrepreneurship cannot be overstated. Entrepreneurship is a risky and uncertain endeavour, and it is impossible to avoid all obstacles and setbacks. However, an entrepreneur who is able to face these challenges head-on and overcome them is more likely to achieve success.

One of the key advantages of overcoming adversity in entrepreneurship is the development of a growth mindset. A growth mindset is the belief that one's abilities and intelligence can be developed through effort and learning.

An entrepreneur with a growth mindset is able to see failure as an opportunity to learn and grow, rather than as a setback. They are also able to view challenges as opportunities for improvement and growth. This mindset enables them to approach problems and setbacks with a positive and proactive attitude.

Another advantage of overcoming adversity in entrepreneurship is the development of resilience.

Resilience is the ability to bounce back from adversity and adapt to changing circumstances. An entrepreneur who is able to develop resilience is able to handle setbacks and failures in a positive manner. They are able to learn from their mistakes and use that knowledge to improve their business. They are able to adapt to changes in the market and find new opportunities.

Overcoming adversity also assists entrepreneurs in fostering a positive attitude, which is vital in the entrepreneurial realm. Entrepreneurs with a positive disposition are able to recognize opportunities and potential, even when others only see hurdles and barriers.

They are able to maintain a hopeful outlook, even in adverse conditions. This optimistic outlook allows them to overcome obstacles and attain great success.

This skill also strengthens entrepreneurs' leadership and team-building abilities. Entrepreneurs who are capable of leading and managing successful teams are more prone to succeed.

Effective leaders inspire and motivate others to join their journey, communicate effectively, foster collaboration and teamwork, and establish a strong support system to help them overcome challenges and achieve success.

Overcoming adversity improves entrepreneurs' strategic thinking skills. Entrepreneurs who can think strategically are able to make informed decisions that lead to success.

They are able to manage risks, set and reach goals, and build a strong support system. They are able to navigate uncertainty and change and uncover new opportunities.

Overcoming adversity also enhances entrepreneurs' marketing and sales strategies. Entrepreneurs who are able to understand and reach their target audience, establish and maintain a strong brand, and develop effective marketing strategies are more likely to succeed.

They can use social media and digital platforms to promote their brand and engage with prospective clients, and they can create effective sales tactics that aid in securing deals and expanding their business.

Furthermore, overcoming adversity can also boost entrepreneurs' creativity and innovation skills. Entrepreneurs who can think creatively and come up with innovative solutions to problems are more likely to succeed. They are able to identify new opportunities and create products and services that fulfil the needs of their target market.

This enables entrepreneurs to identify untapped opportunities and develop products and services that cater to the specific demands of their target audience. As a result, these innovative entrepreneurs are more likely to remain ahead of the competition and achieve success in their business ventures.

Furthermore, overcoming adversity can also help entrepreneurs to develop their ability to navigate and excel in an uncertain and changing business environment. Entrepreneurs who are able to adapt and pivot when necessary are more likely to achieve success.

They are able to anticipate and respond to changes in the market, technology, and consumer behaviour. They are able to identify new opportunities and stay ahead of the curve.

I would like to conclude here that, overcoming adversity is essential to the success of entrepreneurs. Entrepreneurs who are able to overcome adversity are more likely to develop a growth mindset, resilience, a positive attitude, strong leadership and team-building skills, strategic thinking, effective marketing and sales strategies, creativity and innovation, and the ability to navigate an uncertain and changing business environment. These skills and characteristics enable entrepreneurs to overcome obstacles, adapt to changing circumstances, and become real unstoppable entrepreneurs.

Chapter II

Mindset and Attitude

Mindset and attitude are two important factors that can greatly impact an individual's ability to overcome adversity and achieve success. They are closely related concepts, but they have distinct characteristics and functions.

Mindset refers to a person's mental disposition or worldview. It is the way in which an individual sees and interprets the world around them. There are two main types of mindsets: fixed and growth.

A fixed mindset is the belief that one's abilities and intelligence are fixed and cannot be changed. A growth mindset, on the other hand, is the belief that one's abilities and intelligence can be developed through effort and learning.

A growth mindset is essential for entrepreneurs, as it allows them to see failure as an opportunity to learn and grow, rather than as a setback. Entrepreneurs with a growth mindset are able to view challenges as opportunities for improvement and growth, rather than obstacles to be avoided. They are able to approach problems and setbacks with a positive and proactive attitude, which is essential for overcoming adversity.

Attitude refers to a person's emotional and mental state towards a particular situation or object. It is the way in which an individual feels and thinks about something. A positive attitude is essential for entrepreneurs, as it allows them to maintain a positive outlook, even in the face of adversity. A positive attitude allows entrepreneurs to see opportunities and possibilities, even when others see only challenges and obstacles.

For entrepreneurs, a positive attitude is essential for overcoming obstacles and achieving success. It helps entrepreneurs to maintain a sense of optimism and hope, even in the face of adversity. A positive attitude also helps entrepreneurs to stay motivated and focused, which is essential for achieving their goals and succeeding in their venture.

An entrepreneur with a positive attitude is able to handle stress and pressure in a constructive way, rather than becoming overwhelmed or defeated. They are able to maintain a sense of perspective and focus on the bigger picture, rather than getting bogged down in the details. A positive attitude also helps entrepreneurs to build and maintain strong relationships with customers, partners, and employees.

Examples of entrepreneurs who demonstrate a growth mindset and a positive attitude include:

Oprah Winfrey, who faced poverty, abuse, and discrimination early in her life, but she used these experiences to become a stronger and more resilient person. Winfrey has a positive attitude and the ability to think strategically, that has helped her overcome adversity and lead her to success. She is a great example of an unstoppable entrepreneur who has built a strong support system and has the ability to inspire others.

Mark Zuckerberg, the founder and CEO of Facebook, he started Facebook while still a student at Harvard, and has faced numerous challenges and obstacles throughout his career. He has a growth mindset and a positive attitude, which has helped him overcome adversity and achieve success. He is a great example of an entrepreneur who has the ability to think strategically, and has the leadership skills necessary to build and manage high-performing teams.

Mindset and attitude are two important factors that can greatly impact an individual's ability to overcome adversity and achieve success. A growth mindset and a positive attitude are essential for entrepreneurs, as they allow them to see failure as an opportunity to learn and grow, view challenges as opportunities for improvement and growth, maintain a positive outlook, stay motivated and focused, build and maintain strong relationships with customers, partners, and employees, and navigate uncertainty and change with ease.

Developing a growth mindset

Developing a growth mindset is essential for entrepreneurs as it allows them to see failure as an opportunity to learn and grow, rather than as a setback.

A growth mindset is the belief that one's abilities and intelligence can be developed through effort and learning. It is characterized by a willingness to take on new challenges, a desire to learn and improve, and a belief in the power of effort and perseverance.

By embracing a growth mindset, entrepreneurs can cultivate resilience and a willingness to continuously develop themselves, both personally and professionally. This approach can ultimately lead to greater success and fulfilment in both business and life. It encourages individuals to embrace new challenges with enthusiasm. By fostering a growth mindset, entrepreneurs can develop the necessary skills, knowledge, and resilience to overcome adversity and reach new heights of success, both personally and professionally. There are several strategies for developing a growth mindset. Few are given in figure one on next page:

Figure 1: strategies for developing a growth mindset

Strategy	Description
Embrace failure	Failure is a natural part of the learning and growth process. Entrepreneurs who are able to embrace failure and see it as an opportunity to learn and grow are more likely to develop a growth mindset.
Focus on effort, not outcome	A growth mindset is characterized by a focus on effort, not outcome. Entrepreneurs should focus on the process of learning and growing, rather than the end result. By focusing on effort, entrepreneurs are able to see progress and improvement, even when they don't achieve their desired outcome.
Seek feedback	Feedback is essential for learning and growth. Entrepreneurs should seek out feedback from mentors, colleagues, and customers in order to gain new insights and perspectives. Feedback can help entrepreneurs to identify areas for improvement and to make necessary adjustments to their business strategies.
Embrace challenges	A growth mindset is characterized by a willingness to take on new challenges. Entrepreneurs should seek out challenges that will help them to learn and grow. They should view challenges as opportunities for improvement and growth, rather than obstacles to be avoided.
Reflect and learn	Entrepreneurs should take time to reflect on their experiences and to learn from them. They should analyze their successes and failures in order to gain new insights and to identify areas for improvement.

Examples of entrepreneurs who have developed a growth mindset include:

Jeff Bezos, the founder and CEO of Amazon, he has a growth mindset and a willingness to take on new challenges. He has faced numerous challenges throughout his career, and he has used these experiences to learn and grow. He has a strong focus on innovation and customer service, which has helped him to develop new products and services and to improve customer satisfaction.

Elon Musk is a great example of an entrepreneur with a growth mindset. He is constantly pushing the boundaries of what is possible and taking on new challenges. He is not deterred by failure, and he is always looking for ways to improve and innovate. He has faced numerous setbacks and obstacles throughout his career, but he has used these experiences to learn and grow.

Jack Ma, founder and executive chairman of Alibaba Group, he is a great example of an entrepreneur with a growth mindset. He started Alibaba with a small group of friends, and through hard work and perseverance, he has built it into one of the largest e-commerce companies in the world. He has faced numerous challenges throughout his career, but he has used these experiences to learn and grow. He is known for his ability to think strategically and to navigate uncertainty and change.

Ingvar Kamprad, founder of IKEA, he is a great example of an entrepreneur with a growth mindset. He started IKEA with very little money, but through hard work and perseverance, he has built it into one of the largest furniture retailers in the world. He has faced numerous challenges throughout his career, but he has used these experiences to learn and grow.

Steve Jobs, Co-founder of Apple, he is a great example of an entrepreneur with a growth mindset. He started Apple with a small group of friends and through hard work and perseverance he has built it into one of the most valuable companies in the world. Despite facing various obstacles throughout his professional journey, he has utilized them as learning opportunities and opportunities for personal growth. He is recognized for his strategic thinking and his capability to handle change and uncertainty.

Richard Branson, the founder of the Virgin Group, embodies the qualities of a successful entrepreneur with a growth mindset. Starting with a small record store, he has grown the company into a multi-billion dollar conglomerate through determination and hard work. Despite facing numerous obstacles, he has used these experiences as opportunities to learn and improve. Branson is known for his strategic thinking and ability to adapt to uncertainty and change.

These examples show that entrepreneurs with a growth mindset can come from any part of the world, and they have the ability to overcome adversity, adapt to change and achieve success in their venture.

Developing a growth mindset is essential for entrepreneurs as it allows them to see failure as an opportunity to learn and grow, rather than as a setback.

A growth mindset is characterized by a willingness to take on new challenges, a desire to learn and improve, and a belief in the power of effort and perseverance. Embracing failure, focusing on effort, seeking feedback, embracing challenges, and reflecting and learning are some strategies for developing a growth mindset.

Cultivating a positive attitude

Cultivating a positive attitude is essential for entrepreneurs as it allows them to maintain a positive outlook, even in the face of adversity. A positive attitude is characterized by a sense of optimism and hope, a focus on the present and the future, and a belief in one's ability to make a difference. Cultivating a positive attitude can help entrepreneurs to overcome obstacles and achieve success in their venture.

A positive attitude allows entrepreneurs to see beyond current obstacles and envision a brighter future for their venture. It provides them with the motivation and determination to keep pushing forward, even in the face of setbacks or challenges. Furthermore, a positive outlook can help entrepreneurs to remain resilient, stay focused on their goals, and maintain a level of energy and drive that is essential for success.

Additionally, having a positive attitude can also help entrepreneurs to build strong relationships with customers, employees, and partners, and create a positive and productive work environment.

Few key strategies for cultivating a positive attitude are given below in figure 2:

Figure 2: Strategies for cultivating a positive attitude

Strategy	Description
Focus on the present and the future	A positive attitude is characterized by a focus on the present and the future, rather than dwelling on the past. Entrepreneurs should focus on the present moment and on what they can do today to achieve their goals. They should also focus on the future and on the possibilities and opportunities that lie ahead.
Practice gratitude	A positive attitude is characterized by a sense of gratitude and appreciation for what one has. Entrepreneurs should practice gratitude by taking time to appreciate the good things in their life and the people who support them.
Surround yourself with positive people	A positive attitude is contagious, and entrepreneurs should surround themselves with people who have a positive attitude. They should seek out positive role models, mentors, and friends who can inspire and support them.
Practice positive self-talk	A positive attitude is characterized by positive self-talk. Entrepreneurs should practice positive self-talk by replacing negative thoughts with positive ones. This can help them to maintain a positive outlook and to believe in their ability to make a difference.
Keep a positive attitude journal	Entrepreneurs can keep a positive attitude journal where they can write down their thoughts, feelings, and experiences. They can use this journal as a tool to reflect on their progress and to identify areas for improvement.

Examples of entrepreneurs who have cultivated a positive attitude include:

Tony Robbins, an American entrepreneur, author and motivational speaker, he is known for his positive attitude and his ability to inspire and motivate others. He has overcome numerous obstacles throughout his career, but he has used these experiences to learn and grow. He has a strong focus on positive self-talk and the power of the mind to achieve success.

Arianna Huffington, founder of The Huffington Post, she is a great example of an entrepreneur with a positive attitude. She has faced numerous challenges throughout her career, but she has used these experiences to learn and grow. She is known for her ability to maintain a positive outlook, even in the face of adversity.

Cultivating a positive attitude is essential for entrepreneurs as it allows them to maintain a positive outlook, even in the face of adversity. A positive attitude is characterized by a sense of optimism and hope, a focus on the present and the future, and a belief in one's ability to make a difference. Entrepreneurs should focus on the present and the future, practice gratitude, surround themselves with positive people, practice positive self-talk and keep a positive attitude journal. Practicing these strategies can help entrepreneurs to maintain a positive outlook, overcome obstacles, and achieve success in their venture.

Overcoming limiting beliefs

Overcoming limiting beliefs is essential for entrepreneurs as it allows them to break free from self-imposed limitations and achieve their full potential. Limiting beliefs are negative thoughts and self-talk that hold an individual back from achieving their goals. These limiting beliefs can manifest in many forms such as fear of failure, lack of self-confidence, and self-doubt.

By identifying and overcoming these limiting beliefs, entrepreneurs can unleash their full potential, and achieve new levels of success. This involves becoming aware of these negative thought patterns, reframing them into positive and empowering beliefs, and taking action towards their goals despite any fear or self-doubt.

Few key strategies for overcoming limiting beliefs are given on next page in figure 3:

Figure 3: strategies for overcoming limiting beliefs

Strategy	Description
Identify limiting beliefs	The first step in overcoming limiting beliefs is to identify them. Entrepreneurs should take time to reflect on their thoughts and beliefs, and to identify any negative patterns that are holding them back.
Challenge limiting beliefs	Once limiting beliefs have been identified, entrepreneurs should challenge them. They should ask themselves if these beliefs are true and if they are serving them well. They should also consider if there is evidence to support these beliefs and if not, it may be time to let them go.
Reframe limiting beliefs	Once limiting beliefs have been challenged, entrepreneurs should reframe them into positive and empowering thoughts. For example, instead of thinking "I can't do this," entrepreneurs should reframe the thought to "I can learn how to do this."
Develop a growth mindset	A growth mindset is characterized by a belief that one's abilities and intelligence can be developed through effort and learning. Entrepreneurs should develop a growth mindset by embracing failure, focusing on effort, seeking feedback, embracing challenges, and reflecting and learning.
Seek support	Entrepreneurs should seek support from others, such as mentors, coaches or friends, who can provide encouragement and guidance. They can also join support groups or communities, where they can connect with others who share similar experiences and challenges.

Examples of entrepreneurs who have overcome limiting beliefs include:

J. K. Rowling, the author of the Harry Potter series, she faced rejection and rejection from publishers for years, but she refused to let that stop her. She continued to believe in her work and her abilities, and eventually, her book was accepted for publication and went on to become a global bestseller.

Oprah Winfrey, an American media executive, actress, talk show host, and philanthropist, she faced poverty, abuse, and discrimination early in her life, but she refused to let those experiences define her. She developed a growth mindset and a positive attitude, and she used those experiences to become a stronger and more resilient person.

Jack Ma, founder and executive chairman of Alibaba Group, he faced numerous rejections early in his career when trying to secure funding for his company. He was told that the internet would never be a thing in China, but he refused to let that stop him. He believed in his vision and his abilities, and he eventually built Alibaba into one of the largest e-commerce companies in the world.

Ingvar Kamprad, founder of IKEA, he faced numerous rejections when trying to get his furniture designs produced. He was told that his designs were too simple and not good enough, but he refused to let that stop him. He had unwavering faith in his aspirations and capabilities, which ultimately led to the establishment of IKEA as one of the world's biggest furniture retailers.

Richard Branson, founder of the Virgin Group, he faced numerous rejections and obstacles when trying to start his company. He was told that he would never be successful, but he refused to let that stop him. He believed in his vision and his abilities, and he eventually built the Virgin Group into a multi-billion dollar conglomerate.

Sara Blakely, founder of Spanx, she had no experience in fashion or retail, and she faced rejection after rejection when trying to get her product into stores. But she refused to give up, and she eventually found success by selling her product online.

These examples show that entrepreneurs can overcome limiting beliefs and achieve great success in their ventures. They have the ability to see beyond self-imposed limitations, to challenge negative thoughts and beliefs, and to believe in themselves and their abilities.

I would concluded that overcoming limiting beliefs is essential for entrepreneurs as it allows them to break free from self-imposed limitations and achieve their full potential. Limiting beliefs can manifest in many forms such as fear of failure, lack of self-confidence, and self-doubt. Entrepreneurs should identify limiting beliefs, challenge them, reframe them, develop a growth mindset, and seek support. By overcoming limiting beliefs, entrepreneurs can open themselves up to new opportunities, improve their chances of success, and achieve their goals.

It's important to note that overcoming limiting beliefs is a continuous process, it requires constant effort, and self-awareness, it's not a one-time thing, but rather a journey. It's also important to keep in mind that even the most successful entrepreneurs have limiting beliefs, and they work on overcoming them regularly. The key is to be aware of them, acknowledge them and take actions towards changing them to positive beliefs.

Chapter III

Planning and Preparation

Planning and preparation are essential for entrepreneurs as they provide a roadmap for achieving their goals and a framework for decision-making. Planning involves setting specific, measurable, and achievable goals, and identifying the steps and resources required to achieve them. Preparation involves acquiring the knowledge, skills, and resources needed to successfully execute the plan.

Together, planning and preparation provide entrepreneurs with a solid foundation for success. They help to create a clear vision of the future and provide a roadmap for achieving it. They also allow entrepreneurs to make informed decisions, prioritize their actions, and allocate resources effectively. Below are few strategies for planning and preparation in figure 4:

Figure 4: Key strategies for planning and preparation

Strategy	Description
Set specific, measurable, and achievable goals	Entrepreneurs should set specific, measurable, and achievable goals for their venture. These goals should be clear, concise, and aligned with their values and vision. They should also be measurable, so that progress can be tracked and evaluated.
Identify the steps and resources required	Entrepreneurs should identify the steps and resources required to achieve their goals. This can involve conducting market research, identifying target customers, and developing a marketing plan.
Conduct a SWOT analysis	A SWOT analysis is a tool that entrepreneurs can use to identify the strengths, weaknesses, opportunities, and threats of their venture. It can help them to identify the internal and external factors that may impact their success and to develop strategies to mitigate these risks.
Develop a business plan	A business plan is a written document that outlines an entrepreneur's goals, strategies, and resources. It can serve as a roadmap for achieving success and can also be used to secure funding from investors.
Continuously review and adapt the plan	Entrepreneurs should continuously review and adapt their plan as they learn more about the market and their customers. They should be flexible and willing to make adjustments as needed to achieve their goals.

Examples of entrepreneurs who have effectively used planning and preparation include:

Mark Zuckerberg had a clear vision and set specific, measurable and achievable goals for his company. He also identified the steps and resources required and conducted a SWOT analysis to identify potential risks. He also developed a business plan and continuously reviewed and adapted his plan as he learned more about the market and his customers.

Jeff Bezos demonstrated strong leadership by outlining a clear vision for the company and setting achievable goals. He took a methodical approach by determining the necessary steps and resources, analyzing potential risks through a SWOT analysis, and creating a comprehensive business plan. Additionally, he was adaptable by regularly reviewing and adjusting his plan as he gained more understanding of the market and customer needs.

Andrew Forrest, founder of Fortescue Metals Group, he is Australian businessman and philanthropist. He had a clear vision for his company and set specific, measurable, and achievable goals. He also identified the steps and resources required to achieve those goals, and he continuously reviewed and adapted his plan as he learned more about the market and his customers. As a result, he was able to build Fortescue Metals Group into one of the largest iron ore producers in the world.

Eike Batista, a Brazilian businessman, he had a clear vision and set specific, measurable and achievable goals for his company. He also identified the steps and resources required and conducted a SWOT analysis to identify potential risks. He also developed a business plan and continuously reviewed and adapted his plan as he learned more about the market and his customers. He built his company, EBX Group, into one of the largest companies in South America, it was a holding company of several businesses in the fields of oil and gas, mining, shipbuilding and logistics.

Janine Allis, founder of Boost Juice, an Australian businesswoman and entrepreneur. She had a clear vision and set specific, measurable and achievable goals for her company. She also identified the steps and resources required, conducted a SWOT analysis to identify potential risks, and developed a business plan. She also continuously reviewed and adapted her plan as she learned more about the market and her customers. As a result, she was able to build Boost Juice into one of the largest juice bar chains in Australia.

These examples show that entrepreneurs can effectively use planning and preparation to achieve their goals. They have a clear vision, set specific, measurable, and achievable goals, identified the steps and resources required, conducted a SWOT analysis to identify potential risks and developed a business plan. They also continuously reviewed and adapted their plans as they learned more about the market and their customers. By effectively using planning and preparation, entrepreneurs can increase their chances of success and achieve their goals. It's important to note that planning and preparation are not a one-time event, it's a continuous process, and entrepreneurs should always be ready to adapt to the changing market conditions and customer needs.

It is a reality that planning and preparation are vital for entrepreneurs as they provide a roadmap for achieving their goals and a framework for decision-making. Planning involves setting specific, measurable, and achievable goals, and identifying the steps and resources required to achieve them. Preparation involves acquiring the knowledge, skills, and resources needed to successfully execute the plan. By effectively using planning and preparation, entrepreneurs can increase their chances of success.

Setting and achieving goals

Setting and achieving goals is essential for entrepreneurs as it helps them to focus their efforts and to stay motivated. Setting goals involves defining what an entrepreneur wants to achieve, and then creating a plan to achieve it. Achieving goals involves taking action to make progress towards the goal, and making adjustments as necessary.

By setting and achieving goals, entrepreneurs can stay focused on their vision and keep their business moving forward. It helps them to prioritize their efforts, allocate resources effectively, and measure their progress. Achieving small, meaningful goals along the way can also help to build momentum and keep entrepreneurs motivated. Few key strategies for setting and achieving goals are given below in figure 5:

Figure 5: strategies for setting and achieving goals

Strategy	Description
Define what you want to achieve	Entrepreneurs should start by defining what they want to achieve. This can include short-term and long-term goals, as well as specific and measurable objectives.
Create a plan	Entrepreneurs should then create a plan to achieve their goals. This can include identifying the steps and resources required, setting a deadline, and developing a timeline for achieving the goal.
Break down the goal into smaller steps	Entrepreneurs should break down large goals into smaller, more manageable steps. This makes the goal more attainable and allows entrepreneurs to track their progress.
Set deadlines	Entrepreneurs should set deadlines for achieving their goals. Deadlines help to focus efforts and to stay motivated.
Monitor progress and make adjustments	Entrepreneurs should monitor their progress and make adjustments as necessary. This can include revising the plan, seeking feedback, and making changes to the goal or the plan.

Examples of entrepreneurs who have effectively set and achieved goals include:

Elon Musk had a clear vision and set specific, measurable and achievable goals for his company. He also identified the steps and resources required and developed a plan to achieve those goals. He broke down large goals into smaller, more manageable steps, set deadlines, and monitored progress and made adjustments as necessary. As a result, he was able to achieve his goal of launching a reusable rocket into space and to build Tesla into one of the most valuable car companies in the world.

Steve Jobs, the co-founder of Apple, had a clear vision and established specific, measurable, and achievable goals for the company. He also carefully planned and strategized by identifying the necessary steps and resources to reach these objectives. Additionally, he broke down larger goals into more manageable tasks, set deadlines, and continually tracked progress, making adjustments as needed. Through this approach, he was able to successfully revolutionize the personal computer industry and establish Apple as one of the most valuable companies globally.

Tony Elumelu, Nigerian economist, entrepreneur, and philanthropist. He had a clear vision and set specific, measurable and achievable goals for his company. He also identified the steps and resources required, developed a plan to achieve those goals, broke down large goals into smaller, more manageable steps, set deadlines, and monitored progress and made adjustments as necessary. As a result, he built Heirs Holdings, a leading African investment company.

Strive Masiyiwa, a Zimbabwean businessman, entrepreneur and philanthropist, he had a clear vision and set specific, measurable and achievable goals for his company. He also identified the steps and resources required, developed a plan to achieve those goals, broke down large goals into smaller, more manageable steps, set deadlines, and monitored progress and made adjustments as necessary. As a result, he was able to achieve his goal of building Econet Wireless, one of the largest telecommunications companies in Africa.

Mo Ibrahim, Sudanese-British businessman and philanthropist, he had a clear vision and set specific, measurable and achievable goals for his company. He also identified the steps and resources required, developed a plan to achieve those goals, broke down large goals into smaller, more manageable steps, set deadlines, and monitored progress and made adjustments as necessary.

Now the world knows Celtel, one of Africa's leading mobile phone companies.

These examples show that entrepreneurs can effectively set and achieve goals. They have a clear vision, set specific, measurable, and achievable goals, identified the steps and resources required, developed a plan, broke down large goals into smaller, more manageable steps, set deadlines and monitored progress and made adjustments as necessary. By effectively setting and achieving goals, entrepreneurs from Africa and other under-developed countries can increase their chances of success and achieve their goals, despite the challenges.

Identifying and managing risks

Identifying and managing risks is required skill for entrepreneurs as it helps them to anticipate potential problems and to take proactive steps to mitigate those risks. Identifying risks involves identifying the internal and external factors that may impact the success of the venture. Managing risks involves taking steps to mitigate or eliminate those risks.

Some key strategies for identifying and managing risks are given below in figure 6:

Figure 6: strategies for identifying and managing risks

Strategy	Description
Conduct a SWOT analysis	A SWOT analysis is a tool that entrepreneurs can use to identify the strengths, weaknesses, opportunities, and threats of their venture. It can help them to identify the internal and external factors that may impact their success and to develop strategies to mitigate those risks.
Identify the key risks	Entrepreneurs should identify the key risks that may impact their venture. This can include market risks, financial risks, and operational risks.
Develop risk management strategies	Entrepreneurs should develop risk management strategies for each identified risk. These strategies can include diversifying investments, acquiring insurance, and implementing risk management systems.
Continuously monitor and review risks	Entrepreneurs should continuously monitor and review the risks to their venture. They should be prepared to adjust their risk management strategies as needed.
Create a risk management plan	Entrepreneurs should create a risk management plan that outlines the risks identified, the risk management strategies, and the actions that will be taken to mitigate those risks.

Examples of entrepreneurs who have effectively identified and managed risks include:

Ashish J. Thakkar, Rwandan entrepreneur and founder of the Mara Group, he identified the risks involved in starting a business in Africa and took steps to mitigate those risks. He diversified his investments across multiple countries, sectors and industries, so that if one business struggled, the others would continue to perform. He also has a long-term investment strategy which helped him to minimize short-term market fluctuations.

Jenny Morel, founder of Morel & Co., New Zealand based entrepreneur, she identified the risks involved in starting a business and took steps to mitigate those risks. She diversified her investments across multiple sectors and industries and implemented a risk management plan that outlines the risks identified, the risk management strategies, and the actions that will be taken to mitigate those risks.

Warren Buffett, chairman and CEO of Berkshire Hathaway, he is known for his ability to identify and manage risks. He conducts extensive research and due diligence before making investments, and he diversifies his investments to mitigate risk. He also has a long-term investment plan that helps to reduce the impact of short-term market changes.

Mark Zuckerberg identified the risks involved in starting a social network and took steps to mitigate those risks. For example, he created a strong privacy policy to protect user data, and he implemented systems to detect and remove fake accounts and spam.

These examples show that entrepreneurs can effectively identify and manage risks. They conduct extensive research and due diligence, diversify their investments, have long-term investment strategy, and implement risk management plans. By effectively identifying and managing risks, entrepreneurs can make a difference in the success of their business.

Building a strong support system

Building a strong support system is essential for entrepreneurs as it helps them to overcome the challenges they may face and to achieve their goals. A support system can include family, friends, mentors, and professional networks. These individuals and groups can provide emotional, financial, and professional support. Here are a few key strategies for building a strong support system:

Figure 7: strategies for building a strong support system

Strategy	Description
Surround yourself with positive people	Entrepreneurs should surround themselves with positive people who believe in them and their vision. These individuals can provide emotional support and encouragement when things get tough.
Seek out mentors	Entrepreneurs should seek out mentors who have experience and knowledge in the industry. These individuals can provide guidance, advice, and support.
Build a professional network	Entrepreneurs should build a professional network of contacts in their industry. These individuals can provide valuable information, resources, and opportunities.
Seek financial support	Entrepreneurs should seek financial support from family, friends, or investors. This can help to fund the start-up costs and ongoing expenses of the venture.
Join entrepreneur groups	Entrepreneurs should join entrepreneur groups or organizations. These groups provide opportunities to connect with other entrepreneurs and to learn from their experiences.

Examples of entrepreneurs who have effectively built a strong support system include:

Mohammed Dewji, a Tanzanian businessman and philanthropist, He has built a strong support system by surrounding himself with positive people, seeking out mentors, building a professional network, and joining entrepreneur groups. He also receives support from his family and friends, which helped him to achieve his goal of building MeTL Group, one of the largest companies in East Africa.

Muhammad Yunus, Bangladeshi social entrepreneur, banker, economist, and civil society leader, He has built a strong support system by surrounding himself with positive people, seeking out mentors, building a professional network, and joining entrepreneur groups. He also receives support from his family and friends, which helped him to achieve his goal of building Grameen Bank, a pioneer of microfinance and microcredit.

Jack Ma, the founder of Alibaba Group, a Chinese businessman, through his proactive approach, he has surrounded himself with a strong network of supportive individuals who bring positivity and guidance to his life. By seeking out mentors, building a professional network, and participating in entrepreneur groups, he has created a foundation for success that empowers him to reach new heights. He also receives support from his family and friends, which helped him to achieve his goal of building Alibaba Group, one of the largest e-commerce companies in the world.

Shahid Khan, a Pakistani-American entrepreneur, has been successful in creating a strong support system that has helped him reach his goals. This support system includes positive people, mentors, a professional network, and participation in entrepreneur groups. Additionally, his family and friends have been a source of support in his journey, which has resulted in the building of Flex-N-Gate, one of the largest privately held companies in the United States.

At the end of this chapter, I would like to conclude that building a strong support system is important for entrepreneurs as it helps them to overcome the challenges they may face and to achieve their goals. A support system can include family, friends, mentors, and professional networks. These individuals and groups can provide emotional, financial, and professional support.

Entrepreneurs from under-developed and developed countries can increase their chances of success and achieve their goals effectively by building a strong support system,. It is worth noting that building a support system is a continuous process, it requires continuous effort, self-awareness, and adaptability to the changing market conditions and customer needs.

Chapter IV

Resilience and Adaptability

R esilience and adaptability are two key traits that are essential for success among entrepreneurs. Resilience refers to the ability to bounce back from setbacks, challenges, and failures and keep pushing forward. Entrepreneurs who are resilient are able to maintain their optimism and drive even in the face of adversity. Adaptability, on the other hand, refers to the ability to change and pivot quickly in response to shifting market conditions, customer needs, and technological advancements.

Entrepreneurs who are able to adapt quickly and effectively to these changes are better equipped to succeed in an ever-evolving business landscape. By combining resilience and adaptability, entrepreneurs are able to navigate the ups and downs of entrepreneurship and stay on top of the competition.

Here are a few key strategies for developing resilience and adaptability:

Figure 8: strategies for developing resilience and adaptability

Strategy	Description
Develop a growth mindset	Having a growth mindset means embracing challenges, learning from failure, and continuing to grow and improve.
Learn from failure	Failure is a natural part of the entrepreneurial journey. Entrepreneurs should learn from their failures and use that knowledge to improve and move forward.
Be open to change	Entrepreneurs should be open to change and willing to adapt their strategies and plans as needed.
Learn from others	Entrepreneurs should learn from the experiences and strategies of other successful entrepreneurs.
Build a support system	Entrepreneurs should build a support system of family, friends, mentors, and professional contacts who can provide emotional and practical support.

Examples of entrepreneurs who have effectively developed resilience and adaptability include:

Elon Musk has shown resilience and adaptability by embracing challenges, learning from failure, and continuing to grow and improve. He has faced many setbacks and obstacles, but he has always been able to bounce back and continue moving forward, he adapts and changes his strategies and plans as needed.

J. K. Rowling, British author, philanthropist, film producer, television producer, and founder of Harry Potter franchise, she has shown resilience and adaptability by embracing challenges, learning from failure, and continuing to grow and improve. She faced rejection and setback before the Harry Potter series became a success, but she did not give up and continued to write and submit her work. She also demonstrated the ability to adjust and modify her strategies and plans as required.

Muhammad Yunus, Bangladeshi social entrepreneur, banker, economist, and civil society leader, has shown resilience and adaptability by embracing challenges, learning from failure, and continuing to grow and improve. He faced many challenges while building Grameen Bank, but he was able to bounce back and continue moving forward. He also had the ability to change and adjust his plans and strategies as per the requirements of the business.

Wang Jianlin, founder of Dalian Wanda Group, he has shown resilience and adaptability by embracing challenges, learning from failure, and continuing to grow and improve. He faced many challenges while building his conglomerate, but he was able to bounce back and continue moving forward. He also adapted and changed his strategies and plans as needed.

Aliko Dangote, Nigerian businessman, He has shown resilience and adaptability by embracing challenges, learning from failure, and continuing to grow and improve. He faced many challenges while building Dangote Group, one of the largest industrial conglomerates in Africa, but he was able to bounce back and continue moving forward. He is another example of an entrepreneur who adapted and changed his strategies to make business successful.

Mo Ibrahim, a Sudanese-British entrepreneur, philanthropist and the creator of the Mo Ibrahim Foundation, demonstrates determination and flexibility by tackling obstacles, learning from mistakes, and consistently developing and enhancing. Despite facing numerous difficulties during the establishment of his foundation, he was able to recover and persist in his progress. He also modified and adjusted his tactics and objectives as required.

Developing resilience in the face of failure

Resilience is the ability to recover quickly from difficulties or setbacks, both emotional and physical. It is a crucial skill for entrepreneurs, as the path of entrepreneurship often involves a high level of risk and uncertainty, and entrepreneurs are bound to face failures and difficulties along the way. Being resilient means having the mental toughness to overcome challenges and keep pushing forward towards their goals, even when things get tough.

Developing resilience requires a combination of mindset, attitude, and strategies. Entrepreneurs can work on their mindset by cultivating a positive outlook and reframing their perspective on failure. A growth mindset, for example, views failure as an opportunity for learning and growth, rather than as a personal failing.

A healthy attitude and self-care practices, such as exercise and mindfulness, can also help entrepreneurs to stay mentally and emotionally resilient. Entrepreneurs can develop strategies for handling setbacks, such as having a support system, taking regular breaks, and developing a plan for bouncing back after a failure.

Here are a few key strategies for developing resilience in the face of failure:

Figure 9: strategies for developing resilience in the face of failure

Strategy	Description
Embrace failure	Failure is a natural part of the entrepreneurial journey, and entrepreneurs should embrace it as an opportunity to learn and grow.
Learn from failure	Failure is a valuable teacher. Entrepreneurs should take the time to reflect on their failures, identify the mistakes and learn from them.
Have a growth mindset	Entrepreneurs should have a growth mindset and focus on improving and learning from their failures rather than dwelling on them.
Build a support system	Entrepreneurs should build a support system of family, friends, mentors, and professional contacts who can provide emotional and practical support.
Stay motivated	Entrepreneurs should stay motivated and maintain a positive attitude even in the face of failure.

Examples of entrepreneurs who have effectively developed resilience in the face of failure include:

Steve Jobs has shown resilience in the face of failure by embracing failure, learning from it, having a growth mindset, building a support system, and staying motivated. He was fired from Apple, the company he co-founded, but he did not give up and continued to work hard. He also came back to the company and led it to become one of the most successful companies in the world.

Oprah Winfrey, American media executive, talk show host, actress, and philanthropist, she has shown resilience in the face of failure by embracing failure, learning from it, having a growth mindset, building a support system, and staying motivated. She faced many challenges and setbacks early on in her career, but she did not give up and continued to work hard. She also adapted and changed her strategies and plans as needed.

Roshaneh Zafar, Pakistani social entrepreneur and founder of Kashf Foundation, She has shown resilience in the face of failure by embracing failure, learning from it, having a growth mindset, building a support system, and staying motivated. She faced many challenges while building Kashf Foundation, but she was able to bounce back and continue moving forward by changing plans and strategies as per the requirements of the ground realities.

It is important to understand that developing resilience in the face of failure is required for entrepreneurs, as it helps them to bounce back from difficult situations and to continue moving forward. Failure is a natural part of the entrepreneurial journey and it is important for entrepreneurs to be able to handle it in a constructive and effective way. Resilience can be developed through a combination of mindset, attitude, and strategies such as embracing failure, learning from it, having a growth mindset, building a support system, and staying motivated.

Learning from mistakes and setbacks

Learning from mistakes and setbacks is very important for entrepreneurs, as it helps them to improve and to avoid making the same mistakes in the future. Entrepreneurs must be willing to admit their mistakes and to learn from them. This process of learning and growth is an essential part of the entrepreneurial journey.

It is a continuous process of growth and development for entrepreneurs. It requires a growth mindset, a willingness to be vulnerable, and a commitment to continuously improving. Below are key strategies for learning from mistakes and setbacks given in figure ten:

Figure 10: strategies for learning from mistakes and setbacks

Strategy	Description
Reflect on mistakes and setbacks	Entrepreneurs should take the time to reflect on their mistakes and setbacks, identify the causes and learn from them.
Keep a learning journal	Entrepreneurs should keep a learning journal to record their mistakes and setbacks, as well as the lessons they've learned.
Seek feedback	Entrepreneurs should seek feedback from others, such as mentors or colleagues, to gain a different perspective on their mistakes and setbacks.
Be open to learning from others	Entrepreneurs should be open to learning from the experiences and strategies of other successful entrepreneurs.
Don't be afraid to try again	Entrepreneurs should not be afraid to try again, even if they have failed before.

However, it is not the mistake itself that is important, but rather the lessons that can be learned from it. By taking the time to reflect on what went wrong and what could have been done differently, entrepreneurs can gain valuable insights that can help them to improve and avoid making the same mistakes in the future.

Examples of entrepreneurs who have effectively learned from mistakes and setbacks include:

Richard Branson, founder of Virgin Group, he has shown the ability to learn from mistakes and setbacks by reflecting on them, seeking feedback, being open to learning from others, and not being afraid to try again. He has made many mistakes and faced many setbacks throughout his career, but he has always been able to learn from them and continue moving forward.

Jeff Bezos has shown the ability to learn from mistakes and setbacks by reflecting on them, seeking feedback, being open to learning from others, and not being afraid to try again. Despite facing numerous difficulties and obstacles throughout his professional journey, he has consistently demonstrated the ability to learn from them and persist in his progress.

Elon Musk has shown the ability to learn from mistakes and setbacks by reflecting on them, seeking feedback, being open to learning from others, and not being afraid to try again. Throughout his professional journey, he has encountered numerous obstacles and encountered numerous setbacks, however, he has always been able to take valuable lessons from these experiences and press on in his progress. He is not afraid of taking risks and trying again, which has led to the success of SpaceX and Tesla.

Aliko Dangote has shown the ability to learn from mistakes and setbacks by reflecting on them, seeking feedback, being open to learning from others, and not being afraid to try again. Despite facing numerous roadblocks and obstacles throughout his professional path, he has always been able to extract valuable lessons and continue his forward momentum. He has used the knowledge gained from his mistakes and setbacks to improve and grow his business.

Hence, learning from mistakes and setbacks is very important for entrepreneurs, as it helps them to improve and to avoid making the same mistakes in the future.

Entrepreneurs must be willing to admit their mistakes and to learn from them. This process of learning and growth is an essential part of the entrepreneurial journey. By effectively learning from mistakes and setbacks, entrepreneurs from under-developed and developed countries can increase their chances of success and achieve their goals, despite the challenges they may face.

Adapting to change and uncertainty

Adapting to change and uncertainty is essential for entrepreneurs, as it helps them to navigate the constantly evolving business environment. Entrepreneurs must be able to adapt to changes in the market and industry, as well as unexpected events and challenges. Adaptability is a key trait for entrepreneurs as it helps them to be proactive and to make strategic decisions.

Entrepreneurs must be able to recognize changes in their industry, market, or environment, and respond in a proactive and strategic manner. This requires a certain level of agility and flexibility, as well as a willingness to take calculated risks and pivot quickly when necessary. Adaptability also involves the ability to be creative and think outside the box, as well as the ability to effectively communicate and collaborate with team members and stakeholders.

Here are a few key strategies for adapting to change and uncertainty:

Figure 11: strategies for adapting to change and uncertainty

Strategy	Description
Stay informed	Entrepreneurs should stay informed about the latest developments in their industry and market, as well as global events that may affect their business.
Be flexible	Entrepreneurs should be flexible and open to changing their strategies and plans as needed.
Anticipate change	Entrepreneurs should anticipate change and be prepared for unexpected events and challenges.
Be proactive	Entrepreneurs should be proactive and take action to adapt to changes in the market and industry.
Develop a contingency plan	Entrepreneurs should develop a contingency plan to help them navigate unexpected events and challenges.

Examples of entrepreneurs who have effectively adapted to change and uncertainty include:

Masayoshi Son, founder and CEO of SoftBank Group, he has shown the ability to adapt to change and uncertainty by staying informed, being flexible, anticipating change, being proactive, and developing a contingency plan. He has faced many challenges and unexpected events throughout his career, but he has always been able to adapt and continue moving forward.

Abdulla Al Futtaim, owner of Al-Futtaim Group, he has shown the ability to adapt to change and uncertainty by staying informed, being flexible, anticipating change, being proactive, and developing a contingency plan. Throughout his career, he has encountered numerous obstacles and unforeseen circumstances, yet he has consistently demonstrated the ability to adjust and progress. He has successfully diversified Al-Futtaim Group's business portfolio, which has helped the company to adapt to changing market conditions.

I would like to conclude that adapting to change and uncertainty is essential for entrepreneurs, as it helps them to navigate the constantly evolving business environment. Entrepreneurs must be able to adapt to changes in the market and industry, as well as unexpected events and challenges. By effectively adapting to change and uncertainty, entrepreneurs from under-developed and developed countries, especially from the Middle East, can increase their chances of success and achieve their goals, despite the challenges they may face.

Chapter V

Creativity and Innovation

C reativity and innovation are well valued skills for entrepreneurs, as they allow them to come up with new and unique ideas that can lead to the development of new products, services, and business models. Entrepreneurs who are able to innovate and think creatively are able to differentiate themselves from their competitors and create a competitive advantage.

Entrepreneurs who are able to stay ahead of the curve and continuously innovate are better equipped to succeed in such an environment. This requires not just creativity, but also an ability to assess market trends, understand customer needs, and collaborate effectively with team members and stakeholders.

Being creative and innovative, entrepreneurs become in position to differentiate themselves from their competitors, create a competitive advantage, and continuously drive their business forward in an ever-evolving business landscape. Figure 12 presents key strategies for fostering creativity and innovation:

Figure 12: strategies for fostering creativity and innovation

Strategy	Description
Encourage a culture of creativity and innovation	Entrepreneurs should create an organizational culture that encourages employees to think creatively and to come up with new innovative ideas.
Embrace new technologies and advancements	Entrepreneurs should be open to new technologies and advancements and look for ways to incorporate them into their business.
Think outside the box	Entrepreneurs should be willing to think outside the box and consider unconventional solutions and ideas.
Be open to experimentation and failure	Entrepreneurs should be open to experimentation and be willing to try new things, even if they may fail.
Collaborate and network	Entrepreneurs should collaborate and network with other entrepreneurs, experts, and industry leaders to gather new ideas and perspectives.

Examples of entrepreneurs who have effectively fostered creativity and innovation include:

Elon Musk has shown the ability to foster creativity and innovation by encouraging a culture of creativity and innovation, embracing new technologies, thinking outside the box, being open to experimentation and failure, and collaborating and networking. He has been able to create new and unique products and services that have disrupted traditional industries.

Mark Zuckerberg has demonstrated his capacity for fostering creativity and innovation through promoting a culture that values these traits, embracing new technologies, embracing unconventional thinking, being accepting of experimentation and failure, and fostering collaboration and networking. Through his unique and inventive approach, he has enabled individuals to connect and exchange information in a new way, completely transforming how we communicate and share information.

Encouraging creativity and innovation

Encouraging creativity and innovation are very important entrepreneurial abilities for entrepreneurs to come up with new and unique ideas that can lead to the development of new products, services, and business models. Entrepreneurs who are able to encourage a culture of creativity and innovation are able to differentiate themselves from their competitors and create a competitive advantage.

Figure 13 on next page highlights few key strategies for encouraging creativity and innovation:

Figure 13: strategies for encouraging creativity and innovation

Strategy	Description
Foster a diversity of perspectives	Entrepreneurs should encourage a diverse team of employees, with different backgrounds, experiences, and perspectives, as diverse perspectives can lead to more innovative ideas.
Encourage experimentation and risk-taking	Entrepreneurs should encourage experimentation and risk-taking, even if it means the possibility of failure. Failure can be an opportunity to learn and improve.
Encourage continuous learning and growth	Entrepreneurs should encourage continuous learning and growth, as new knowledge and skills can lead to new and innovative ideas.
Provide resources for innovation	Entrepreneurs should provide resources, such as time, money, and technology, for employees to pursue new and innovative ideas.

Examples of entrepreneurs who have effectively encouraged innovation and out-of-the-box thinking include:

Mo Ibrahim, Sudanese-British businessman, and philanthropist, he has shown the ability to encourage creativity and innovation by encouraging a culture of creativity and innovation, embracing new technologies, thinking outside the box, being open to experimentation and failure, and collaborating and networking. He has innovatively devised methods to enhance good governance and leadership in Africa through his foundation.

Jack Ma has shown the ability to encourage creativity and innovation, through a diversity of perspectives, encouraging experimentation and risk-taking, encouraging continuous learning and growth, and providing resources for innovation. He has been able to create a new and unique business model that has disrupted traditional e-commerce and online marketplaces.

Mohammed Dewji, the CEO of MeTL Group, has exhibited his ability to promote creative thinking and innovation by creating a culture that values creativity and innovation, promoting diversity of ideas, encouraging experimentation and embracing risk, promoting ongoing learning and growth, and providing resources for innovation. He has introduced new and novel ways of running the business, leading to the flourishing of MeTL Group.

Leveraging technology and digital tools

Leveraging technology and digital tools are very important skills for entrepreneurs. These skills allow them to streamline their operations, reach a wider audience, and stay competitive in today's digital landscape. Entrepreneurs who are able to effectively leverage technology and digital tools are able to improve their efficiency and effectiveness, and gain a competitive advantage in the market.

The entrepreneurs can automate repetitive tasks, manage their operations remotely, and collect and analyze data to make informed business decisions by leveraging technology and digital tools,. These tools also provide entrepreneurs with the ability to reach a wider audience through digital marketing and social media, and to collaborate with team members and customers from anywhere in the world.

Here are a few key strategies for leveraging technology and digital tools:

Figure 14: strategies for leveraging technology and digital tools

Strategy	Description
Stay up to date with the latest technology	Entrepreneurs should stay informed about the latest technology trends and advancements, and look for ways to incorporate them into their business.
Invest in digital tools	Entrepreneurs should invest in digital tools such as CRM software, project management software, and marketing automation software to improve their operations and reach a wider audience.
Use social media and online platforms	Entrepreneurs should use social media and online platforms to reach a wider audience, promote their brand, and connect with customers.
Implement automation	Entrepreneurs should implement automation where possible, such as automated marketing campaigns, to improve their efficiency and effectiveness.
Embrace data analytics	Entrepreneurs should embrace data analytics to gain insights into customer behaviour and make data-driven decisions.

Examples of entrepreneurs who have effectively leveraged technology and digital tools include:

Mark Zuckerberg has shown the ability to leverage technology and digital tools by staying up to date with the latest technology, investing in digital tools, using social media and online platforms, implementing automation, and embracing data analytics. He has been able to create a new and unique way for people to connect and share information, which has changed the way we communicate and share information.

Njeri Rionge, Founder and Chair of Ignite Consulting, She has shown the ability to leverage technology and digital tools by staying up to date with the latest technology, investing in digital tools, using social media and online platforms, implementing automation, and embracing data analytics. She has been able to leverage technology and digital tools to grow her business and reach a wider audience. She has used digital tools to streamline her operations and automate tasks, and has used social media and online platforms to promote her brand and connect with customers. She has also embraced data analytics to gain insights into customer behaviour and make data-driven decisions.

Jack Ma has shown the ability to leverage technology and digital tools by staying up to date with the latest technology, investing in digital tools, using social media and online platforms, implementing automation, and embracing data analytics. He has been able to create a new and unique business model that has disrupted traditional e-commerce and online marketplaces.

In under-developed countries, entrepreneurs are leveraging technology and digital tools to overcome the lack of infrastructure and resources. For example, M-Pesa, a mobile banking service in Kenya, is a great example of how technology can be leveraged to provide financial services in areas where traditional banking infrastructure is lacking. This service allows individuals to make payments and transfer money using their mobile phones, making it easier for people to access financial services in under-developed regions.

Cultivating a culture of creativity

Cultivating a culture of creativity is vital for entrepreneurs, as it allows them to generate new ideas, solve problems, and stay competitive in the marketplace. Entrepreneurs who are able to foster a culture of creativity are able to differentiate themselves from their competitors and create a competitive advantage.

A culture of creativity refers to an organizational environment that encourages and supports creative thinking and innovation. This type of culture values new ideas, encourages employees to challenge the status quo, and provides opportunities for experimentation and risk-taking.

In addition to its impact on the development of new ideas and solutions, a culture of creativity can also have a positive impact on employee morale and engagement. When employees feel valued and encouraged to be creative, they are more likely to be satisfied with their work and to be more committed to the success of the organization.

Here are a few key strategies for cultivating a culture of creativity:

Figure 15: strategies for cultivating a culture of creativity

Strategy	Description
Encourage divergent thinking	Entrepreneurs should encourage their employees to think outside the box and consider different perspectives and ideas.
Provide resources for creativity	Entrepreneurs should provide resources such as time, money, and technology for employees to pursue new and innovative ideas.
Foster a culture of experimentation	Entrepreneurs should foster a culture of experimentation and encourage employees to take risks and try new things.
Encourage continuous learning and growth	Entrepreneurs should encourage continuous learning and growth, as new knowledge and skills can lead to new and innovative ideas.
Reward creativity	Entrepreneurs should reward employees for their creative contributions, such as new ideas and solutions.

Examples of entrepreneurs who have effectively cultivated a culture of creativity include:

Elon Musk has demonstrated a strong ability to cultivate a culture of creativity by encouraging divergent thinking, providing resources for creativity, fostering a culture of experimentation, encouraging continuous learning and growth, and rewarding creativity. He has been able to create new and unique products and services that have disrupted traditional industries.

Mark Zuckerberg is also an example of showing the ability to cultivate a culture of creativity by encouraging divergent thinking, providing resources for creativity, fostering a culture of experimentation, encouraging continuous learning and growth, and rewarding creativity. He has been able to create a new and unique way for people to connect and share information, which has changed the way we communicate and share information.

Mo Ibrahim is another example of entrepreneurs who have shown the ability to cultivate a culture of creativity by encouraging divergent thinking, providing resources for creativity, fostering a culture of experimentation, encouraging continuous learning and growth, and rewarding creativity. He has been able to create new and unique ways to promote good governance and leadership in Africa through his foundation.

In under-developed countries, entrepreneurs are also cultivating a culture of creativity to overcome the lack of resources and infrastructure. For example, in Africa, some entrepreneurs are using technology and innovation to create new business models and products that addresses the lack of infrastructure and resources. For instance, in Kenya, some entrepreneurs are using mobile technology to provide financial services in areas where traditional banking infrastructure is lacking. They are using creativity and innovative solutions to create new ways of doing business that can help to improve people's lives and contribute to the development of the country.

I would like to conclude that cultivating a culture of creativity is very important for entrepreneurs, as it allows them to generate new ideas, solve problems, and stay competitive in the marketplace. By encouraging divergent thinking, providing resources for creativity, fostering a culture of experimentation, encouraging continuous learning and growth, and rewarding creativity, entrepreneurs from under-developed and developed countries can increase their chances of success and achieve their goals, despite the challenges they may face.

Chapter VI

Leadership and Team

Building

Leadership and team building are essential for entrepreneurs, as they play a crucial role in the success of a business. Entrepreneurs who are able to effectively lead and build a strong team are able to create a positive work environment, improve employee morale, and achieve their goals.

Leadership is the ability to guide, inspire and motivate others to achieve a common goal. A good leader is able to clearly communicate their vision and goals, and provide direction and guidance to their team.

They lead by example, setting a positive tone for the company culture and modelling the behaviour and values that they expect from their employees. Good leaders are also able to build trust and respect among their team members, and are able to resolve conflicts and misunderstandings.

Team building is the process of creating a cohesive and motivated team that works together towards a common goal. A strong team is made up of individuals with different skills and perspectives, who are able to work together effectively to achieve their objectives.

Leadership and team building are especially important for entrepreneurs, as they are often responsible for creating and leading a team from the ground up. Entrepreneurs who are able to effectively lead and build a team are able to create a positive work environment, improve employee morale, and achieve their goals.

These entrepreneurs need to be able to create teams that are diverse, inclusive, and empowering, to foster a culture of innovation and creativity, and to inspire employees to work together to achieve common goals.

Here are a few key strategies for leadership and team building given in figure 16:

Figure 16: strategies for leadership and team building

Strategy	Description
Lead by example	Entrepreneurs should lead by example and set a positive tone for the company culture. This means that they should model the behaviour and values that they expect from their employees.
Communicate effectively	Entrepreneurs should communicate effectively with their employees, providing clear guidance and direction. This means that they should be able to clearly articulate their vision and goals, and provide regular updates on the progress of the business.
Empower employees	Entrepreneurs should empower employees to take ownership of their work and make decisions. This means that they should give their team members the resources and authority they need to complete their tasks, and should also trust them to make decisions that are in the best interest of the business.
Build trust	Entrepreneurs should build trust with their employees by being transparent and consistent in their actions. This means that they should be honest and open about the business to build good trust.
Encourage collaboration	Entrepreneurs should encourage collaboration among employees to promote teamwork and the sharing of ideas. This means that they should create opportunities for employees to work together, and should also recognize and reward the contributions of team members.

Examples of entrepreneurs who have effectively demonstrated leadership and team building include:

His Highness Sheikh Mohammed bin Rashid Al Maktoum, Vice President and Prime Minister of the United Arab Emirates is a great example of leading by example, communicating effectively, empowering employees, building trust, and encouraging collaboration. He has created a strong and united team that has contributed in the development of Dubai as well as in the development of the UAE.

Richard Branson, founder of the Virgin Group, he has shown the ability to lead by example, communicate effectively, empower employees, build trust, and encourage collaboration. He has been able to create a strong and united team that has contributed to the success of the Virgin Group.

Naguib Sawiris, an Egyptian businessman and billionaire, he has shown the ability to lead by example, communicate effectively, empower employees, build trust, and encourage collaboration. He has been able to create a strong and united team that has contributed to the success of his companies.

In under-developed countries, entrepreneurs are also focusing on leadership and team building to overcome the lack of resources and infrastructure. For example, in Africa, some entrepreneurs are using leadership and team building to create a positive work environment, improve employee morale, and achieve their goals. For instance, some entrepreneurs are using leadership and team building to create teams that are diverse, inclusive, and empowering, to foster a culture of innovation and creativity, and to inspire employees to work together to achieve common goals.

Developing leadership skills

There are several approaches that entrepreneurs can take to develop their leadership skills:

1) **Self-reflection:** Entrepreneurs should take the time to reflect on their own strengths and weaknesses as a leader. This can involve self-evaluation exercises and journaling, where entrepreneurs can identify areas where they excel and areas where they need

improvement. By reflecting on their own performance, entrepreneurs can set personal and professional development goals that will help them to grow as leaders.

2) **Mentorship:** Entrepreneurs can seek out mentors who have experience and expertise in leadership and business. These mentors can provide guidance, advice and feedback, as well as serve as a sounding board for entrepreneurs. Entrepreneurs can learn from the successes and failures of their mentors and apply what they learn to their own leadership style.

3) **Education and training:** Entrepreneurs can invest in leadership development programs, workshops, or classes. These can provide them with the knowledge and skills needed to become an effective leader, such as communication, decision making, problem solving, and emotional intelligence. These programs can also provide entrepreneurs with opportunities to network with other leaders and learn from their experiences.

4) **Reading and research:** Entrepreneurs can read books, articles, and research on leadership and management to gain new insights and ideas. This can help entrepreneurs to stay up-to-date on the latest

leadership theories and best practices, and can also provide them with inspiration for their own leadership style.

5) **Practice:** Entrepreneurs can practice their leadership skills by leading teams or taking on leadership roles in volunteer organizations or non-profits. This can provide entrepreneurs with hands-on experience in leading and motivating others, and can also provide them with valuable feedback on their leadership style.

6) **Embrace Failure:** Failure is an opportunity to learn, and a good leader should embrace this opportunity to grow. Entrepreneurs should learn to accept failure as a learning opportunity, and use it to improve their leadership skills. By learning from their mistakes, entrepreneurs can develop a more resilient and adaptive leadership style.

7) **Build a Strong Network:** Building a strong network of contacts can be a powerful tool in developing leadership skills. Entrepreneurs should seek out individuals who can provide advice, guidance and support as they develop their leadership skills. This can include other leaders, mentors, and peers. A strong

network can also provide entrepreneurs with new ideas and opportunities.

8) **Empower Others:** Entrepreneurs should empower their team members to take ownership of their work and make decisions. By doing this, entrepreneurs will learn how to delegate tasks effectively, and will develop trust and respect among their team members. Empowering others can also help entrepreneurs to build a more resilient and adaptable team, which is essential for long-term success.

Ultimately, developing leadership skills takes time and effort, and requires a commitment to ongoing learning and self-improvement. Entrepreneurs should be willing to invest time and resources into developing their leadership skills, and be open to feedback and new ideas.

Building and managing high-performing teams

Building and managing high-performing teams is crucial for any business that wants to achieve success. A team that works well together, is motivated and engaged, and has a clear sense of direction and purpose, can help to overcome challenges, achieve goals and drive innovation. In this section, we will explore some of the best approaches for building and managing high-performing teams.

These include setting clear roles and responsibilities, hiring the right people, effective communication, setting goals, encouraging teamwork, providing training and development opportunities, recognizing and rewarding team members, leading by example, creating a flexible team, and encouraging innovation and creativity. These approaches when implemented effectively will help to create a strong and productive team that can drive the success of any business.

1) **Clearly Define Roles and Responsibilities:** It is crucial to clearly define the roles and responsibilities of each team member. This will help to ensure that everyone is on the same page, and that everyone knows what is expected of them.

2) **Hire the Right People:** Building a high-performing team starts with hiring the right people. This means to look for the individuals who possess the skills,

experience and attitude to fit in with the team and help to achieve the company's goals.

3) **Communicate Effectively:** Clear and open communication is essential to building and managing a high-performing team. This means regularly holding team meetings, providing regular updates and feedback, and encouraging team members to share their ideas and concerns.

4) **Set Goals and Objectives:** Setting clear and measurable goals and objectives can help to keep the team focused and motivated. This can help to build a sense of purpose and direction, and can also help to ensure that everyone is working towards the same end goal.

5) **Encourage Teamwork:** High-performing teams are made up of individuals who work well together. Entrepreneurs should encourage teamwork by fostering an environment where team members feel comfortable sharing their ideas, and where they feel valued and respected.

6) **Provide Training and Development Opportunities:** Providing team members with training and development opportunities can help to improve their

skills and knowledge. This can help to keep team members motivated and engaged, and can also help to improve the overall performance of the team.

7) **Recognize and Reward:** Recognizing and rewarding team members for their hard work and achievements can help to build morale and motivation. This can include things like bonuses, promotions, or public recognition.

8) **Lead by Example:** Entrepreneurs should lead by example, setting the tone for the team culture and modelling the behaviour and values that they expect from their employees. This can help to create a positive work environment, and can also help to build trust and respect among team members.

9) **Create a Flexible Team:** High-performing teams are adaptable and flexible. Entrepreneurs should be open to new ideas and willing to make changes when necessary. This can help to create a more resilient and adaptive team, which is essential for long-term success.

10) **Encourage innovation and creativity:** Encourage team members to think creatively and come up with new ideas. This can help to foster a culture of innovation

within the team and can lead to new solutions and new ways of working.

In conclusion, building and managing high-performing teams requires a combination of effective leadership, clear communication, and a focus on the development of each team member. Entrepreneurs should be willing to invest time and resources into building a strong team, and be open to feedback and new ideas in order to achieve success.

Communication and collaboration

Effective communication and collaboration are key elements in building and managing high-performing teams. Effective communication promotes transparency, trust, and understanding among team members, while collaboration allows for the pooling of resources, knowledge, and ideas to achieve a common goal. Here are some strategies for communication and collaboration that entrepreneurs can implement in their teams:

1) **Establish clear and regular channels of communication:** Entrepreneurs should establish clear and regular channels of communication that allow for

the flow of information and ideas among team members. This includes regular team meetings where updates on projects, progress, and issues can be discussed, and weekly or daily check-ins to ensure that everyone is on the same page. Additionally, open-door policies should be implemented so team members can approach the leader with any concerns or questions they may have.

2) **Encourage active listening:** Team members should be encouraged to actively listen to one another, and to be open to feedback and new ideas. This can be achieved by promoting a culture of mutual respect, where team members are encouraged to speak up and share their thoughts, and where feedback is given and received in a constructive manner. Active listening improves the team's ability to collaborate and make better decisions.

3) **Use technology to facilitate communication and collaboration:** Technology can be a great facilitator of communication and collaboration among remote or dispersed teams. This includes video conferencing, instant messaging, and project management tools that

allow team members to communicate and collaborate in real-time, regardless of their location.

4) **Encourage transparency and honesty:** Transparency and honesty are essential in building trust among team members. These are key values to effective communication and collaboration. Entrepreneurs should encourage team members to share their thoughts and ideas openly, and to be transparent about their intentions, expectations, and goals.

5) **Foster a culture of collaboration:** Entrepreneurs should foster a culture of collaboration by encouraging team members to work together, and by recognizing and rewarding the contributions of team members. This can be achieved by creating opportunities for team members to collaborate on projects and tasks, and by creating a sense of shared ownership of the team's goals and objectives.

6) **Establish a clear decision-making process:** Effective communication and collaboration depend on having a clear decision-making process that team members can rely on. Entrepreneurs should establish a process that is transparent, inclusive, and allows everyone to contribute. This includes giving team members the

opportunity to provide input on important decisions, and making sure that everyone understands the decision-making process and their role in it.

7) **Encourage diversity:** Teams that include a diverse group of individuals with different backgrounds, perspectives, and skill sets tend to be more innovative and productive. Entrepreneurs should strive to create a diverse team and to encourage the participation of all team members. This includes actively recruiting individuals from different backgrounds and providing training and development opportunities that help to build an inclusive culture.

8) **Encourage face-to-face communication:** While technology can be a great facilitator of communication and collaboration, it's important to remember that face-to-face communication is still the most effective way to build trust and understanding. Entrepreneurs should encourage team members to meet in person, whether it is for team-building activities or for important discussions, as this can help to build stronger relationships and improve communication.

9) **Assign a communicator:** Assigning a team member to be in charge of communication can help to ensure that

everyone is on the same page, and that important information is not lost in translation. This includes making sure that team members are informed of project updates, deadlines, and any other important information in a timely manner.

10) **Continuously evaluate and improve:** Entrepreneurs should continuously evaluate the communication and collaboration strategies and make adjustments as necessary to improve the team's performance. This includes regularly collecting feedback from team members, analyzing communication patterns and identifying areas for improvement, and making adjustments to the communication and collaboration.

Here are some specific examples to highlight the key strategies for leadership and team building:

Sheikh Ahmed bin Saeed Al Maktoum, Founder and CEO of the Emirates Group, is an example of an entrepreneur who leads by example. He is known for his strong work ethic, his commitment to excellence, and his integrity. He sets a positive tone for the company culture by modelling the behaviour and values that he expects from his employees. He has played a key role in the growth and success of the Emirates Group and his leadership serves as an inspiration for many.

Prince Alwaleed bin Talal, founder of Kingdom Holding Company, is also an example of an entrepreneur who leads by example. He is known for his strong work ethic, his commitment to excellence, and his integrity. He sets a positive tone for the company culture by modelling the behaviour and values that he expects from his employees.

Lubna Olayan, CEO of Olayan Financing Company, is an also example of an entrepreneur who communicates effectively. She is known for her ability to clearly articulate her vision and goals, and for her willingness to listen to feedback and concerns from her employees. She is also good at providing regular updates on the progress of the business by considering the employees' perspective in this regard.

Waleed Almogbel, CEO of Al-Rajhi Bank, is an example of an entrepreneur who encourages collaboration among employees. He creates opportunities for employees to work together and recognizes and rewards the contributions of team members. He also fosters a culture of collaboration and is open to new and innovative ideas.

He has encouraged a sense of companionship and collective purpose within the group, empowering them to work together towards a shared goal. Through his support and guidance, he has enabled each individual to fulfil their potential and strive for excellence. His enthusiasm and passion for the project have been infectious - inspiring others to go beyond what they thought was possible. As a result, the team has achieved remarkable successes that were once considered out of reach. He also provided much-needed motivation during difficult times and always kept morale high with his cheerful demeanour.

Mohamed Alabbar, Chairman of Emaar Properties, is also an example of an entrepreneur who encourages collaboration among employees. He creates opportunities for employees to work together and recognizes and rewards the contributions of team members. He also fosters a culture of collaboration and is open to new and innovative ideas. His actions have helped to improve the quality of work and build a sense of community and shared purpose among team members.

I would like to conclude that leadership and team building are essential elements of any successful business.

Strong leadership and a cohesive team can help entrepreneurs to overcome challenges, achieve their goals, and create a positive work environment. Entrepreneurs who are able to effectively lead and build a team are able to create a positive work environment, improve employee morale, and achieve their goals, in any part of the world.

Chapter VII

Sales and Marketing

Sales and marketing are necessary components of any business, and are crucial for the success of entrepreneurs. The term "sales" refers to the process of identifying, attracting, and acquiring customers, while marketing is the process of promoting and positioning a product or service to potential customers. Together, sales and marketing help to generate revenue and drive growth for a business.

The importance of sales for entrepreneurs lies in the fact that it is the process through which a business generates revenue and profits. Without sales, a business cannot survive, as it is through sales that a business is able to attract and retain customers. Entrepreneurs need to be able to identify potential customers, understand their needs and preferences, and develop effective strategies to attract and retain them.

Marketing, on the other hand, is essential for building awareness and interest in a business's products or services. It helps to create a positive image and reputation for a business, and helps to differentiate it from its competitors. Marketing also helps to identify and understand target markets, and to develop effective strategies to reach and engage with them.

Both sales and marketing are essential for entrepreneurs because they help to generate revenue and drive growth for a business. Entrepreneurs who are able to effectively generate leads, convert them into customers, and retain those customers will be better positioned to succeed. Additionally, by understanding target markets and developing effective strategies to reach and engage with them, entrepreneurs will be able to build awareness and interest in their business, and differentiate themselves from competitors.

Understanding and reaching your target market

Understanding and reaching your target market is crucial for the success of any business, and entrepreneurs must take the time to understand their target market in order to effectively market and sell their products or services. Target market refers to the specific group of consumers that a business is trying to reach and serve. By understanding and reaching your target market, entrepreneurs can create effective marketing strategies that resonate with their target market, and ultimately generate more revenue.

One key aspect of understanding your target market is identifying their demographics. Demographics include information such as age, gender, income, education level, and occupation. By understanding the demographics of your target market, entrepreneurs can create marketing campaigns and products that are tailored to the specific needs and preferences of their target market. For example, a business that targets young professionals may create a marketing campaign that emphasizes the convenience and flexibility of their products or services, while a business that targets retirees may focus on the durability and reliability of their products.

Another important aspect of understanding your target market is to understand their psychographics. Psychographics refer to the attitudes, values, interests, and lifestyles of a target market. By understanding the psychographics of your target market, entrepreneurs can create marketing campaigns that resonate with their target market on an emotional level. For example, a business that targets environmentally-conscious consumers may create a marketing campaign that emphasizes the eco-friendly features of their products or services, while a business that targets health-conscious consumers may focus on the nutritional benefits of their products.

In addition to understanding your target market, entrepreneurs must also take the time to reach their target market. This can be done through various marketing channels such as social media, email marketing, search engine optimization, and traditional advertising. Entrepreneurs should consider the specific needs and preferences of their target market when selecting marketing channels. For example, a business that targets older consumers may find that traditional advertising such as print or television is more effective, while a business that targets younger consumers may find that social media is more effective.

Reaching target market in underdeveloped countries is a bit different than developed countries, as the infrastructure and access to technology might be limited. Entrepreneurs should be creative and resourceful in identifying ways to reach their target market, for example by using more traditional methods such as word-of-mouth or door-to-door marketing. In addition, entrepreneurs should also consider cultural differences and tailor their messaging and marketing efforts accordingly.

Here are few situations to illustrate the concepts further:

A clothing retailer in the United Arab Emirates (UAE) realized that their target market was primarily made up of young, fashion-conscious consumers. They understood that these consumers were heavily influenced by social media, so they decided to focus their marketing efforts on

Instagram and Facebook. They created a strong social media presence, and used influencers to promote their brand. This helped to increase brand awareness and drive sales among their target market.

A technology company in Pakistan wanted to reach small businesses in rural areas. They realized that these businesses were unlikely to have access to the internet, so they decided to use traditional marketing methods such as word-of-mouth and door-to-door sales. They also created a network of local resellers who could provide on-site support and training to small businesses in these areas. This helped them to successfully reach and serve their target market.

A food delivery service in Saudi Arabia was struggling to reach and serve its target market of busy, working professionals. They realized that these consumers were unlikely to have the time or inclination to search for food delivery options online. They decided to focus their marketing efforts on targeted advertising and promotions through popular messaging apps, such as WhatsApp and Telegram, which are widely used in the region. This helped them to increase brand awareness and drive sales among their target market.

An e-commerce platform in Africa was struggling to reach and serve its target market of cost-conscious consumers. They realized that these consumers were unlikely to have access to credit cards, so they decided to focus on mobile payments and cash on delivery options. They also created a network of local payment providers and partners, which helped them to reach and serve their target market.

In all of these cases, the businesses were able to successfully reach and serve their target market by understanding their specific needs and preferences and tailoring their marketing efforts accordingly. These case studies demonstrate the importance of understanding and reaching your target market, and the impact it can have on the success of a business.

Building and maintaining a strong brand

Building and maintaining a strong brand is crucial for the success of any business, and entrepreneurs must take the time to create and maintain a strong brand in order to effectively differentiate themselves from their competitors. A brand refers to the overall perception and reputation that a business has in the minds of its customers and the public. A strong brand can help to create trust and loyalty among customers, and can ultimately drive more sales and revenue.

One key aspect of building a strong brand is creating a consistent brand identity. This includes creating a logo, colour scheme, and messaging that are consistent across all touch points of a business, such as websites, social media, and marketing materials. By creating a consistent brand identity, entrepreneurs can create a strong visual representation of their brand that is easily recognizable and memorable. For example, Coca-Cola's logo, colour scheme, and messaging are consistent across all touch points, which helps to create a strong and recognizable brand identity.

Another important aspect of building a strong brand is creating a strong brand promise. A brand promise refers to the value or benefit that a business promises to deliver to its customers. By creating a strong brand promise, entrepreneurs can create a clear and compelling message that resonates with their target market. For example, FedEx's brand promise is "When it absolutely, positively has to be there overnight," which clearly communicates the value and benefit that their customers can expect from their services.

In addition to building a strong brand, entrepreneurs must also take the time to maintain and protect their brand. This includes monitoring and managing their online reputation, responding to customer complaints and feedback, and protecting their intellectual property. Entrepreneurs should also be aware of cultural and legal differences when building and maintaining a brand in different countries.

Reaching and building a strong brand in underdeveloped countries can be challenging as the market is not as mature as developed countries, and the infrastructure and access to technology might be limited. Entrepreneurs should be creative and resourceful in identifying ways to reach their target market, for example by using more traditional methods such as word-of-mouth or door-to-door marketing. In addition, entrepreneurs should also consider cultural differences and tailor their messaging and marketing efforts accordingly.

To sum up, building and maintaining a strong brand is crucial for the success of any business. Entrepreneurs must create and maintain a consistent brand identity, create a strong brand promise, and maintain and protect their brand. Building and maintaining a brand in underdeveloped countries and Middle East can be challenging as the market is not as mature as developed countries, and entrepreneurs should consider cultural and legal differences. A strong brand can help to create trust and loyalty among customers, and can ultimately drive more sales and revenue.

Here are a few strategies for building and maintaining a strong brand:

Figure 17: strategies for building and maintaining a strong brand

Strategy	Description
Define your brand's unique value proposition	Identify what sets your brand apart from your competitors and communicate this clearly in your messaging and marketing efforts.
Create a consistent brand identity	Develop a logo, colour scheme, and messaging that are consistent across all touch points of your business. This will help to create a recognizable and memorable brand identity.
Build a strong online presence	Establish a strong online presence through social media and a professional website. This will help to increase brand awareness and establish trust with your target market.
Be authentic and transparent	Be authentic and transparent in your branding and communication. This will help to create trust and loyalty among your customers.
Listen and respond to customer feedback	Monitor and respond to customer feedback, complaints, and reviews. This will help to identify areas for improvement and maintain a positive brand reputation.
Protect your intellectual property	Protect your brand by trade marking your logo and name, and also by monitoring for potential infringement.
Leverage Influencers	Partner with Influencers in your industry or niche to promote your brand and increase brand awareness.
Localize your brand	If you are targeting a specific region, consider tailoring your branding and messaging to align with cultural and religious customs.

By following these strategies, entrepreneurs can effectively build and maintain a strong brand that resonates with their target market and differentiates them from their competitors.

Here are a few examples of case studies that illustrate the strategies for building and maintaining a strong brand:

A coffee shop in Dubai wanted to create a strong brand identity and differentiate themselves from competitors. They defined their unique value proposition as offering high-quality, ethically-sourced coffee. They created a consistent brand identity by using a specific colour scheme and logo, and developed a strong online presence through social media and a professional website. They also made sure to highlight their ethical sourcing practices in all of their messaging and marketing efforts. As a result, they were able to establish a strong and recognizable brand identity that resonated with their target market of coffee lovers.

A fashion e-commerce platform in Saudi Arabia wanted to build a strong brand and increase sales. They leveraged the popularity of social media in the region by partnering with local influencers to promote their brand.

They also created a consistent brand identity by using a specific colour scheme and logo, and developed a strong online presence through social media and a professional website. They also listened and responded to customer feedback by offering a wide range of sizes and styles to cater to different customers. As a result, they were able to increase brand awareness and drive sales among their target market of fashion-conscious consumers.

An online education platform in Pakistan wanted to establish a strong brand and increase enrolment. They defined their unique value proposition as providing affordable, high-quality education to students in rural areas. They created a consistent brand identity by using a specific colour scheme and logo, and developed a strong online presence through social media and a professional website. They also made sure to highlight their commitment to affordable education in all of their messaging and marketing efforts. They also protected their intellectual property by trade marking their logo and name. As a result, they were able to establish a strong and recognizable brand identity that resonated with their target market of students in rural areas.

A software company in Africa wanted to establish a strong brand and increase sales. They leveraged the popularity of mobile payments in the region by offering a range of payment options, including mobile payments and cash on delivery. They also created a consistent brand identity by using a specific colour scheme and logo, and developed a strong online presence through social media and a professional website. They also made sure to tailor their messaging and marketing efforts to align with cultural customs and religious beliefs. As a result, they were able to establish a strong and recognizable brand identity that resonated with their target market of cost-conscious consumers.

These case studies demonstrate the importance of defining a unique value proposition, creating a consistent brand identity, building a strong online presence, and being authentic and transparent. They also show how listening to customer feedback and tailoring branding to align with cultural customs and religious beliefs is crucial when building and maintaining a brand in underdeveloped countries and Middle East. By following these strategies, businesses can effectively build and maintain a strong brand that resonates with their target market and differentiates them from their competitors.

Developing effective marketing strategies

Developing effective marketing strategies is crucial for the success of any business, and entrepreneurs must take the time to research and understand their target market in order to create marketing campaigns that will be most effective. Marketing refers to the process of planning and executing the conception, pricing, promotion, and distribution of ideas, goods, and services to create exchanges that satisfy individual and organizational objectives.

One key aspect of developing effective marketing strategies is conducting market research. This includes researching your target market, identifying their needs and wants, and understanding their purchasing behaviours. Entrepreneurs should also conduct competitor research in order to understand how their competitors are positioning themselves in the market and identify any gaps in the market that they can fill.

Another important aspect of developing effective marketing strategies is creating a unique value proposition (UVP). A UVP is a clear and compelling statement that communicates the unique value that your business offers to its customers. By creating a UVP, entrepreneurs can create a clear and compelling message that resonates with their target market and differentiates their business from their competitors.

When developing a marketing strategy in underdeveloped countries, entrepreneurs should be aware of the limited infrastructure and access to technology, which may make it difficult to reach their target market. Entrepreneurs should be creative and resourceful in identifying ways to reach their target market, for example by using more traditional methods such as word-of-mouth or door-to-door marketing. In addition, entrepreneurs should also consider cultural differences and tailor their marketing efforts accordingly.

Some tips for the entrepreneurs to develop effective marketing strategy are given in figure 18 available on next page:

Figure 18: Tips for the entrepreneurs to develop effective marketing strategy

Tips	Description
Conduct thorough market research	Understand your target market, their needs and wants, and their purchasing behaviours. This will help you identify the gaps in the market that you can fill with your products or services.
Create a unique value proposition (UVP)	Develop a clear and compelling statement that communicates the unique value that your business offers to its customers. This will help you create a clear and compelling message that resonates with your target market and differentiates your business from your competitors.
Develop a marketing mix	Consider the 4 P's of marketing - product, price, place, and promotion - and how they work together to create a cohesive and effective marketing strategy.
Be creative and resourceful	Identify ways to reach your target market that may not be as traditional, such as word-of-mouth or door-to-door marketing.
Tailor your marketing efforts	Consider cultural and religious differences, and tailor your marketing efforts accordingly. Understanding cultural and religious differences will help you create marketing campaigns that are more effective.
Be aware of local laws and regulations	Understand local laws and regulations, and make sure that your marketing strategies comply with them.
Leverage technology	In underdeveloped countries, where the market is not as mature as developed countries, entrepreneurs should leverage technology to reach their target market.
Measure and evaluate	Measure and evaluate the effectiveness of your marketing strategies, and adjust them as necessary.

In addition to market research and creating a UVP, entrepreneurs must also take the time to develop a marketing mix that includes the 4 P's of marketing: product, price, place, and promotion. The product refers to the goods or services that a business offers. The price refers to the cost of the product or service. The place refers to where the product or service is sold. The promotion refers to how the product or service is marketed. Entrepreneurs must consider how these elements work together to create a cohesive and effective marketing strategy.

I would like to conclude that Sales and Marketing are both essential for entrepreneurs to generate revenue and drive growth for a business. Sales help to identify, attract, and acquire customers, while marketing helps to promote and position a product or service to potential customers. Together they help to create a positive image and reputation for a business, and differentiate it from its competitors. Entrepreneurs who understand and effectively implement both sales and marketing strategies will be better positioned for success.

Chapter VIII

Conclusion

This book delves into the topic of becoming an unstoppable entrepreneur by focusing on strategies for overcoming adversity and achieving success. The book begins by defining what it means to be an unstoppable entrepreneur and the importance of overcoming adversity in entrepreneurship. It then goes on to explore key areas that entrepreneurs need to focus on to develop a mindset and attitude that will enable them to overcome any obstacle and achieve success.

The book then covers the importance of planning and preparation in entrepreneurship, which includes setting and achieving goals, identifying and managing risks, and building a strong support system. The book also covers the importance of resilience and adaptability in entrepreneurship, which includes developing resilience in the face of failure, learning from mistakes and setbacks, and adapting to change and uncertainty.

The book also explores the importance of innovation and creativity in entrepreneurship, which includes encouraging innovation and out-of-the-box thinking, leveraging technology and digital tools, and cultivating a culture of creativity. The book also covers leadership and team building, which includes developing leadership skills and building and managing high-performing teams.

The book also covers the importance of sales and marketing for entrepreneurs, which includes understanding and reaching your target market, building and maintaining a strong brand, and developing effective marketing strategies. The book concludes by highlighting the importance of communication and collaboration as well as the importance of leveraging technology and data to make informed decisions.

Throughout the book, the reader is presented with definitions, examples, and case studies from underdeveloped countries and developed world to help them better understand the concepts and strategies discussed. The book is written with the aim of providing entrepreneurs with the tools and knowledge they need to overcome adversity and achieve success in their entrepreneurial pursuits.

Summing up key takeaways

Summing up the key takeaways from this book, entrepreneurs can become unstoppable by:

1) Developing a growth mindset and cultivating a positive attitude.

2) Overcoming limiting beliefs and focusing on solutions rather than problems.

3) Planning and preparing thoroughly by setting and achieving goals, identifying and managing risks, and building a strong support system.

4) Being resilient and adaptable in the face of failure, learning from mistakes and setbacks, and adapting to change and uncertainty.

5) Encouraging innovation and out-of-the-box thinking, leveraging technology and digital tools, and cultivating a culture of creativity.

6) Developing leadership skills, building and managing high-performing teams, and focusing on communication and collaboration.

7) Understanding and reaching your target market, building and maintaining a strong brand, and developing effective marketing strategies.

8) Measuring and evaluating the effectiveness of your strategies and making adjustments as necessary.

In addition, it is important to consider cultural and religious differences and tailor your strategies accordingly, as well as being aware of local laws and regulations. It is also important to leverage technology and data to make informed decisions. By focusing on these key takeaways, entrepreneurs can become unstoppable and achieve success in their entrepreneurial pursuits.

The Future of Entrepreneurship

The future of entrepreneurship looks bright, as more and more people are recognizing the potential of starting their own businesses to achieve financial freedom and create innovative solutions to societal problems. The strategies and concepts discussed in this book provide a valuable framework for entrepreneurs to navigate the challenges and opportunities of the future.

One key area that will continue to be important for entrepreneurs is the ability to adapt to change and uncertainty. As technology continues to rapidly advance and global markets become more interconnected, entrepreneurs will need to be agile and able to pivot their business strategies as necessary. This includes being open to new technologies and digital tools, as well as being willing to enter new markets and explore new business models.

Another important aspect for the future of entrepreneurship is the need to focus on sustainability and social impact. Consumers and investors are increasingly looking for businesses that prioritize environmental and social responsibility, and this trend is likely to continue in the future. Entrepreneurs who can demonstrate their commitment to making a positive impact on society and the environment will be well-positioned to succeed.

Another future trend that entrepreneurs need to be aware of is the growing importance of data and analytics. As more data is generated, it will become increasingly important for entrepreneurs to be able to analyze and use this data to make informed decisions. Entrepreneurs who are able to leverage data and analytics to gain insights into customer behaviour and market trends will be better equipped to anticipate changes and make strategic decisions.

Also, in the light of the recent pandemic, the trend of digitalization and e-commerce is increasing rapidly. Entrepreneurs have to be prepared for the changes that come with the time, digitization brings a lot of opportunities to reach a wider audience, and to be more flexible and efficient in the way of working. In the future, entrepreneurs who are able to effectively navigate the digital landscape will have a significant advantage over their competitors.

Furthermore, with the current global trend of remote working, it's becoming increasingly important for entrepreneurs to be able to lead and manage remote teams effectively. This requires strong communication and collaboration skills, as well as the ability to use digital tools and platforms to keep team members connected and engaged.

In addition, in the light of the current economic and political landscape, it's becoming increasingly important for entrepreneurs to be able to navigate complex regulations and political systems. This includes understanding local laws and regulations, as well as being aware of political and economic trends that may affect their business.

The future of entrepreneurship is filled with opportunities and challenges. Entrepreneurs who are able to adapt to change and uncertainty, prioritize sustainability and social impact, leverage data and technology, and navigate complex regulations and political systems will be well-positioned to succeed. The strategies and concepts discussed in this book provide a valuable framework for entrepreneurs to navigate the future and achieve success in their entrepreneurial pursuits.

About the Author

Rashed Saqer Obaid Al Dhaheri is a successful entrepreneur who has a proven track record of success in a culturally diverse environment. Throughout his career, he has demonstrated an unwavering commitment to promoting creativity and innovation, embracing new technologies and thinking outside the box to find new and better ways of doing things. With a passion for continuous learning and growth, Rashed has proven time and again that he has a spirit of unstoppable entrepreneur, always pushing himself and those around him to reach new heights.

As a proud UAE national with a combination of local and global outlook, Rashed has a deep understanding of the cultural landscape and has been able to effectively navigate and lead in a culturally diverse environment. With a strong foundation in professional education and a commitment to research and learning, he is always looking for new and innovative ways to improve himself and his organizations.

With a name meaning "person with integrity on the right path" in Arabic, Rashed places a strong emphasis on living with honesty and strong moral principles, both in his personal and professional life.

Rashed's educational background spans from early education to post-graduate studies, and he is currently pursuing a professional doctorate in the field of Artificial Intelligence (AI) and planning for the future livelihood of youth in the UAE from the perspective of public sector employees. Rashed's commitment to integrity, education, and professional growth sets him apart and makes him a valuable asset to any organization.

Rashed is a true inspiration to those around him, embodying integrity, honesty, and strong moral principles in both his personal and professional life. With his professional background in Abu Dhabi government and private sector, he has made a lasting impact on the organizations he has been associated with, leading them to new levels of success and growth. As a leader, he encourages and fosters creativity, innovation, and continuous learning, inspiring others to reach their full potential.

With his extensive experience working in culturally diverse environments, Rashed has developed a unique perspective and the ability to understand and bring together different perspectives, skills and experiences to drive creative and innovative solutions. He is passionate about sharing his knowledge and experiences with others and helping them solve the problems they face in their entrepreneurial journey. This combination of skills and drive make him a valuable resource for anyone looking to succeed in the world of entrepreneurship.

www.ingramcontent.com/pod-product-compliance
Lightning Source LLC
Chambersburg PA
CBHW071136220526
45467CB00015B/1190